BOUNDLESS

BOUNDLESS

Poetry by
LAWRENCE KLEIN

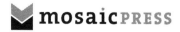

Library and Archives Canada Cataloguing in Publication

Title: Boundless / poetry by Lawrence Klein.
Names: Klein, Lawrence, author.
Identifiers: Canadiana (print) 2024032367X | Canadiana (ebook) 20240323688 | ISBN 9781771617765 (softcover) | ISBN 9781771617772 (PDF) | ISBN 9781771617789 (EPUB) | ISBN 9781771617796 (Kindle)
Subjects: LCGFT: Poetry.
Classification: LCC PS8621.L444 B68 2024 | DDC C811/.6—dc23

Published by Mosaic Press, Oakville, Ontario, Canada, 2024.
MOSAIC PRESS, Publishers
www.Mosaic-Press.com
Copyright © Lawrence Klein, 2024

Printed and bound in Canada.

MOSAIC PRESS
1252 Speers Road, Units 1 & 2, Oakville, Ontario, L6L 2X4 (905)-825-2130
info@mosaic-press.com • www.mosaic-press.com

Are Words Our Masters
or Are They Our Slaves

DEDICATION

Synchronicity is when a random event
Is linked together to create a 'God Sent'
Outcome: When in retrospect no one could know
That in 2003 the American Psychiatric meeting in Toronto
Would lead to dinner with Howard Aster, publisher of Mosaic Press
With a guest, Poet Irving Layton, regaled us with great excess
He recounted a tale of being in court with three ex-wives,
And each had a lawyer, in Solomon's legal guise.
On leaving, I recited my Poem, with great panache,
Irving's back handed complement was, 'An Intellectual Ogden Nash'!
I then wrote Irving a poem, regaled by his performance at dinner.
Little did I know it would result in making me a winner
Of notoriety, as my poem was found in his file labeled 'my favorite',
After his passing; Concordia U. asked, "Could they publish it in his 'obit'.
I replied: 'Of course'. Then, Sixteen years later, Mosaic Press gave me a call,
Asking if they could publish my Poetry! I replied, YES - ALL

I must acknowledge four + major influences in my last 50 years.

- As Co-Founder of Thought Technology, with Dr. Hal Myers, we've become a Worlds leading manufacturer of #Biofeedback / #Neurofeedback since 1974, we've unlocked Human Potential in a hundred Medical Applications, Peak Performance in Sports, the Arts, Education, and Business.

- As Co-Author of the "Mind Over Muscle" Peak Performance Biofeedback Program, in 1974, with Major Nory Laderoute, Athletic Director of Canadian Armed Forces Combat Training Center, we've worked with tens of thousands of Olympic and professional Athletes in over 80 Countries.

- As Co-Founder of The Biofeedback Federation of Europe educational society with Dr. Erik Peper, Professor at San Francisco University, we've shared the knowledge of hundreds of experts in Psychophysiology, Biofeedback & Neurofeedback with many thousands of Clinical Experts since 1995.

- The inspiration for this book is my remarkable wife Dr. Janet Shinder, who has not only delivered over 11,000 Babies, but also our two exceptional Children, Talia (means Heaven's Dew) and Ariella (means lioness of God). Ironic that their names fit their personalities perfectly.

The meaning of life is to see the silver lining in everything that 'fate delivers' – you will read this in my poetry.

PREFACE

My writing poetry started in 1972: after Meditating an hour a day for three months, Poems were 'delivered whole'! I jumped up and 'transcribed' them in 60 seconds, as I feared forgetting what had been 'delivered'! I was completely stunned, as it was unexpected, and I had never ever written poetry.

Forty Eight years later, I was reading a book on Mindfulness, and to my shock, it explaining my first three Poems! It said: René Descartes's "I think therefore I am" in his Discourse on Method (1637) was his first step in demonstrating the attainability of certain knowledge! The first rebuttal of this idea came 300 years later, when Jean-Paul Sartre replied: "Consciousness is not possible 'in Words'"! I had an "Ah-Ha" moment, as it elegantly explaining the meaning & logic behind my first 3 Poems. It had never occurred to me! My 4th poem was kind of "transcendental explanation to 'assuage my guilt'" I surmise, for using words, to explain consciousness. Thus, my poems explain Meditation, Breathing, & Mindfulness.

INTRODUCTION

The Romantic poet William Blake, like Jacob, wrestled angels. As a visionary, he dined and talked with Isaiah and Ezekiel. And he said...

"Exuberance is beauty"
and
"Improvement makes strait roads, but the crooked roads without Improvement, are roads of Genius".

These proclamations have been the lifelong operating principles for my brother Lawrence, who sadly was lost to us two years ago. Larry's poems were wrestled from his life and contain not one but two rebirths. They reflect his intuitions, discoveries, beliefs and visceral reactions to hard won truths. He believed that if you said Yes to Life, life could not possibly say No. Faith can move mountains perhaps; it will also write celebratory poetry.

Freedom was his central value and, when not writing poetry, he helped to develop many biofeedback devices to provide freedom from medications, so that everyone might have new tools to control their inner lives without dependency or habituation. He developed treatments for chronic pain, anxiety, smoking, weight loss, insomnia and a host of other problems where shining an inner light could be freeing. Where one might see a web, Larry would see a net. And devise an exit.

His poetry reflects his exuberance. Language can be a net; but with ingenuity the escape route can be found. Creativity, imagination, innovation are all celebrated in his poems... the right brain! – not the wrong brain. The deep mind, not the monkey mind. You can start by wriggling out of the traps set by conventional thoughts and pedestrian words but now you must leap into the not yet known.

William Blake also said, "Eternity is in love with the productions of time." And Larry believed exactly this, although his sayings were perhaps somewhat more earthbound... "Whoever dies with the most toys, wins." And "You're only young once, but you can be immature forever." The trick was to never relinquish wonder and joy in life, agreeing with Nietzsche that the definition of maturity was "to have reacquired the seriousness that one had as a child at play." He said "toys" but he meant "joys". As a result there were serious poems to celebrate the productions of time. But there also were poems for every family occasion.

Birthdays, graduations, weddings, anniversaries, any and all transitions brought rhyming stanzas, quatrain memories to be shared amongst everyone. The muse, I heard told, would put her phone on silent at night because Larry might call at any hour. He mistrusted words but loved to communicate! And he would cook up a goulash of memory, relationships, happenstance and playful rhapsody. Anybody could do that once. Larry did it a thousand times.

This whole-hearted assent becomes a kind of ascent – a journey of obstacles surmounted and joyful repatriation. Are Words our masters or our slaves?... They become steppingstones – our companions and our emissaries. And so Larry's poems, making use of wonder and gratitude, succeed in creating a coterie of like-minded spirits. A book that starts with internment and isolation makes its way to joy in family, work, human citizenship, and wandering among the hundreds of billions of galaxies – (perhaps ours being "more equal" than others) – and reading with scrupulous amazement the scripture of DNA.

Psychology was his base for interrogating experience, but that led to Larry musing on larger questions of rapture and repose... the exhilaration of downhill skiing, rollerblading, windsurfing, parachuting and, once in a while, driving too fast. All these activities have in common some element of what Einstein denoted "free fall." That condition in which a freely falling body is weightless and so is equivalent to a body floating in space, completely released from the constraints of gravity. To master weightlessness and know yourself in it was behind both his body's impulse and his poetic impulse.

Year in, year out I sat on his right hand at our family's Passover meal, the Seder. Being older, I sat closer to the head of the table. His hearing in his right ear, over many years, had begun to fail. We would be in deep conversation, Larry's point of view always readily available. Whatever the discussion, I would say everything twice since Larry would unfailingly have to turn so that his left ear was beside me and we would together try to decide whether what I had to say was worth the discomfort of the 180° turn.

But siblings often must turn to hear each other. And so...

We retold the fable of escape from slavery, each one of us reading a part in turn, a story that is universal and shared throughout so many cultures and communities. Captivity, yearning, memory and struggle... these are universal themes to which Larry, in his poems, adds his personal voice.

-Jack Klein

1. WORDS

Words Words Words TICTALK TICTALK TicTalk TI
Talk TICTALK TICTALK TICTALK TicTalk TI
Blah Blah Blah Blah Blah Blah Words Words
TicTalk TicTalk SPEECH Thought TicTalk TI
Words Language TICTALK TICTALK TicTalk TI
Language SPEECH Thought TICTALK TicTalk
Reflection Words Dispute Duality Deba
Words WORDS Words Blah Blah Blah Blah
Blah BlahBlah Blah Blah Blah Blah Words Words Wo
Words Language SPEECH Thought
TikTalk TIKTALKTIKTALK
BLAHBLAH BLAH BLAH Deba
eflection Dispute Duality ENCLOSE
WORDS Words Word Words Wo
ords Words Words Word DS WORDS
Talk TICTALK TICTALK TICTALK TICTALK
on Dispute Duality ENCLOSURE
Language SPEECH Thou Blah BLAH
ah BlahBlah BlahBlah AHBLA

WORDS

Are words our masters, or are they our slave?
A hopeless conundrum, but let me save
You from this riddle. For it is only speech,
Internal and externalized which requires the reach

For definitions of ideas, conceptions, and thought
Which are inherent to mankind, and need not be taught.
But words are not plastic, but rigid and fixed,
And it matters not how they are mixed,

they still must mean what the dictionary said,
and they structure the ideas that go on in your head.
So, until you slip their slippery noose
And really let your mind go loose,

to wander through emotion, sensation and space,
you'll never understand, the meaning of grace.

DESCARTES AND SARTRE

Philosopher René Descartes,
Said, "I think therefore I am" start
a conversation within your mind
for self realization. But that kind

of thought Jean-Paul Sartre
said three hundred years later; "Words" aren't
in the Present, but the "Past" and "Future",
to "Be here now, do not endure

language". For Words will just enslave
Your Mind with puzzles, so do save
your equanimity. Enable peace and soul to rest,
in the here and now, I can attest.

Breath out for six seconds and in for four,
Relax your Mind and Body to the Core.

MEDITATION

It is impossible for logic,
Whatever the pedagogic
discipline, to transcend
the chains of self. To pretend that
linear thought
which begot,
the dichotomy, is equal to the task,
to unmask,
the riddle of consciousness,
one must confess,
is illogical. Ego projects riddles to transcend,
and without end,
poses
and reposes,
questions to amuse the self. It is a paradox,
one can't outfox.
To seek the self from within,
Quiet must transcend the conscious din.

2. BARS

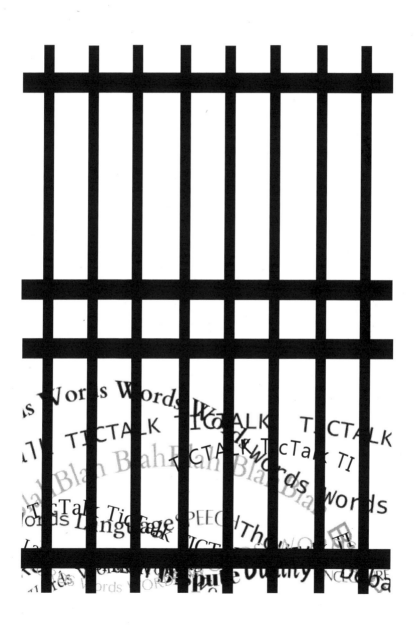

Spending 369 days as "The Guest of the Dutch Government" system, I spent the first 9 months in 3 houses of detention, and then the last 3 months in a Prison. The benefit of this sojourn was I began to write Poetry after 90 days of Meditation. I had graduated from University with a BA with a major in Psychology, and had practiced Meditation there. This was an ideal circumstance to focus on that practice. Having an International Certification as a Ski Coach & Instructor, I also had an opportunity to do Yoga and focus on my Physical Fitness, despite being in a Six sq meter cell. Ironic that after 10 years I received a Canadian Government Pardon, and 46 years after my conviction it's now 100% legal. But I broke the law and did my time.

PRISON POETRY

Oh, I wish it could be for a heroic deed that I go to Jail,
Patriotism, democracy even the crown and then I'd surely rail
Against injustice, tyranny, or antimonarchical swine,
Regrettably, money spoils the otherwise surely crime.
Altruism untarnished is surely the highest deed,
To raise levels of consciousness is fine, but oh that dreaded greed,
Well, money aside the act itself is one that's truly fine,
The incidental wealth must be borne tasting like quinine.

Imagine a world of people on pot, and then envisage war,
With water pistols and colored balloons without the cannons roar.
An economical devastation which must never come to pass,
If Jesus saw this eventuality, he'd surely say the last mass.

Shoot the dirty swine, they're challenging our power,
Disrupting society, corrupting our youth with their cries of Flower
Power to the people, and put an end to strife. Smoking hash
Is a political crime, people smuggle so all can have stash.

'DOING TIME'

Time exists the same for us all
Only it's easier when you're not in jail,
The hours drag and mind begins to pall,
Depression sets in and your sense of humour fail.

Well, if you want to giggle come with me,
And explore the world of absurdity.
A group of criminals languish for years
Because they like cannabis rather than beers

Or liquor, wine or whatever you choose
we tax it and profit, so better drink booze.
A violent society needs pleasure which
Will vent aggression, so better not switch,

'cause hash and pot make you mellow and think
Of beauty, serenity, values and our link
With all mankind. The force used to deal
With this innocuous substance we must appeal.
The waste in lives for a plant so sublime
Is the price we pay for society's crime.

BARS

Bars on the windows, Bars on the doors,
Bars on the ceiling, Bars on the floors,
A Skinner box experiment with men 'stead of rats,
We'll change your behavior, societies' 'tit for tats.'

There was no victim, there was no crime,
Sentence one year, with our countries slime,
We plan to deport you after we're done,
Punishment first, then out on your bun.

But count your blessings like the man said,
You could serve ten - twenty years, even be dead.
When the pressure mounts and the walls close in,
Take heart and know, you've done no sin.

FOREST OF BARS

There's a forest here with bars 'stead of trees,
Which are ignorant of seasons and know no leaves,
They symbolize power and brawn over brain
And serve no purpose save that of pain,

But life all opposites, the antithesis define
the meaning of freedom, for they are a sign,
as villains everywhere they show their hand,
and like all evil are anchored in sand.

The water of time will erase their power,
Nourishing the soul and cause it to flower.
The ebb and flow of the tides of fate
Rise and fall and reiterate,

That each moment must be understood
To transform their iron into wood.

CONVOLUTED GLASS'
'stream of consciousness' / non-poem

Convoluted glass shield the world from my eyes and me from theirs.
Ostriches. Toilet glass* can't hide your cesspool. Iron crosses join
to crucify my freedom. This symbol of sickness chafes incessantly.
A collar constricting my breath and breadth. The chain rattle drips acid
In my ears. Somnolent sailors sailing a soulless sea. Sigh.
For forest, flowers, family, friends, faraway freedom.
Not the word or state but the emotion.
A state of mind. International, universally understood.
As different as mankind yet as identical.
Aspiration which separates and unites, fire which warms and consumes.
The unity of opposites gives meaning as death gives life, pleasure
Pain. Confinement liberty. Scant consolation.
Do time. Mark Time. All in good time.
At the same time. In no time. Have a good time.
Seconds, seasons, centuries, measure and measureless.
Our senses micro and telescope. Motions perception changes in and out
Of the stream. Severed from the world, the square of sky our clock,
Time is an abstraction. An ocean to fill. A fortune to waste. Our
Essence. Our nemesis.
Dehydrated mans thirst for freedom drowning in time.
Burning desire only quenched by time.

* The window was frosted or marbled glass.

'THE BUST'

T'was a sunny morning in May
When the policeman came to take 'em away.
The birds sang, the cows did munch
And the police said they were acting on a hunch

Of a neighbour next door to where I live
Who happened to be a detective.
Two dozen keys of fine black 'Pak'
I scoured my mind to uncover their knack

To come a few hours before the job was done
And turn forty thousand dollars into none.
Nine months I've sat in a 6 sq. meter cell
And each Saturday I hear Vara Hilversum two* tell

The local hashish prices and quality
And I ponder the absurdity.
Are the Judges fools? Is the system insane?
There surely be someone to blame.

Where government commissions favour legalize pot
And inside prisons users and dealers' rot.
At the Nuremberg trials after they legalize,
'We were only following orders' Cops and Judges will cry.

* National Dutch Radio.

THE JUSTICE SYSTEM

Welcome, heh heh, I'm the mad doctor,
Glad we caught your problem in time.
I've got some medicine I know you'll abhor,
It's painful and ineffectual at combatting crime,

But it's the only cure in my big black bag,
Besides, we've been using for hundreds of years.
New fangled cures aren't enough of a drag.
I want repentance, blood, sweat and tears.

Murder, rape, drugs, theft or embezzlement
My remedy is always the same.
Just alter the dosage, enough to make you repent.
So you have problems, am I to blame?

Criminals are getting soft, cures used to be much tougher,
Chopping of hands, heads, or a black hole for years.
Society and I want to see you suffer,
Damn the cost to family and careers.

You come out as you came in, except for the scars.
Ever notice you're almost all lower class?
Laws are made by politicians for the rich which bars
Most poor from advancement. You think the mass

From which you come should share the wealth?
Well get a job. Too bad you have no skills.
Teach you? Hell, you're criminals, go use your stealth
My medicine is PAIN. Education and learning are frills.

I'm not sadistic, besides the laws on my side.
We're too civilized for bullfights but crime gives us the right
For virtuous violence, so you better abide
by my rules. I write them, and justice is might.

ODE TO A 'HUIS VAN BEWARING';
(Dutch house of detention)

The guard wakes me before seven, why I don't know.
So I can sit in my cell, sure makes the day go slow.
At nine there is 'luchten', half an hour of cloud or rain.
Then 'till twelve my six sq meter cell, a miracle I'm not insane.

Cursed potatoes and probably spinach, the one hot meal a day,
Maybe a pudding and always an egg, Vegetarians really pay
The price for their convictions. Perhaps one a month I see
A piece of fruit, and a fresh salad is even a greater rarity.

At two-thirty another half-hour outside, then back into your cage,
'till six and wash up and bread and cheese, enough to make you rage.
Three time a week there is recreation and one and a half hours sport.
And a couple of hours of religious meeting locked inside this fort.

At eleven the lights go out, and then there were no sounds,
Save my breath and sigh while my wild heart pounds,
At the thought of my coming trial and the possibility,
Of then finally passing sentence and thereby set me free,

To leave this senseless dungeon and live in tranquility
In a beautiful prison, which compared to this hell, is pure serenity.

THE SYSTEM

This punitive system fills me with distaste.
Those responsible don't have courage, and must justify
Their violence, dehumanizing, laying lives to waste
Because 'they are only following orders.' It does signify

Their lack of conviction in their action,
For they never defend their deeds, only their authority.
Challenged, they quiver with fear and rage. But it's little satisfaction
Countering a shackled programmed mind with incisive lucidity.

They think might makes right, but they are always wrong
So they must continually assert themselves to prove they exist.
A strict disciplinary system us where they belong.
Time and science have shown that using the fist

To alter behavior does not achieve the goal
Of reshaping individuals to obey the law.
Rehabilitation through self knowledge and study are the sole
Means of reintegrating people who have shown a flaw.

They prattle of new buildings and a fancy - colored cell,
But the crux is their unchanged vengeful mentality.
All they can create is an opulent HELL,
until they start preparing men to be free.

Ceasing treating men like children, making them plead
For creative work, study and play, which is their right.
You lock us in solitary confinement and do not heed
Our human aspirations, that require insight.

In 'The Crime of Punishment' Dr. Menninger states repeatedly
'reformation, not vindictive suffering should be the purpose of treatment'.
Criminology, penology, psychiatry, psychology
Echo this fact; but nothing will change until the element

Of self-righteous vengeance is eliminated.
Violence spawns violence, the dragon remains unsated.

3. REBORN ONCE

"At length for hatchling ripe
he breaks the shell"

Published by Blake : 17 May 1793

WHY!

Ask not why,
Forsooth, because
Between earth and sky
There is sufficient cause
To live or die,

Without knowing. That is, life can be whatever you will,
Live by the sea, or on top of a hill.
Frantic frenetic,
Tranquil ascetic.

Whatever you choose, for choice is a must,
On our brief voyage from seed to dust.
Energy channeled and thought directed,
Stasis is death and life rejected.

Physical reality can be transcended,
For the metaphysical plane projects un-ended.
And all levels of reality are interdependent,
For the life of the spirit is transcendent.

LIFE

Run the race that's never won,
And push yourself just for Fun,
to the brink of exhaustion.

Climb a mountain, explore the Sea,
Values dance and float for they are free,
anchored only in your reality.

Construct a new paradigm
And few thoughts that rhyme,
All competing for longevity. Ah Time,

the master complexity,
Along with the sea,
Will engulf thee!

BEING

Feel your hands, fondle your toes,
Know that in life anything goes
down or up, it's all relative
to where we are now. You must give

thanks for your fortune fate or luck,
good or bad don't mean a fuck,
when you can always start anew
Roll naked in the morning dew

and savor, taste smell hearing sight; and feel
our sexuality should make us kneel
before our maker, and our being,
with all these eyes why is seeing

So difficult. Breathe oh so
slowly. And know
that the universe is within and without,
and without doubt

to love your neighbor you must love yourself.
Peace of mind and joy - your wealth.

RANDOM

Random, is the feet of God in the sands of time.
The mathematical implications are so sublime,
For they presuppose that chance must even out.
There is order in the chaos without a doubt.

DIVINE PROVIDENCE

How does good fortune and God intertwine?
When I am lucky, is that divine
providence? Are earthly concerns any of his?
The retarded child or the whiz kid

Seem randomly to deserve their fate.
Is there love or truth innate?
The justice in order seems akin to mans'.
By what higher law and in who's hands

Do the meek perish and the strong survive?
By what forces do we stay alive?

THERE CAN BE ONLY ONE

There can be only one
Creator under the Sun.
One, of a Billion Stars,
where the planet Mars

is on our doorstep; the One,
whatever our color or tongue,
Source of life unites us all,
when in prayer we call,

with pure heart, suspend thought,
in all religions we are taught
the Divine resides within us all
if we allow our souls to call,

collect, our spirits in one voice
Peace on Earth, is our choice.

4. BOUNDLESS

MEDITATION MEANING

Isn't it strange that in words we can find
Meaning. Meaning? You know the kind
of idea transmittable intact through space
Comprehensible throughout the human race.

What wonder that phonetics are amenable
To idea formulation, so that they're tenable
To be juggled and merged to a conceptual whole
And mirror the complexity of our soul.

MEDITATION'S SECRET — BREATHING

Traveling at the speed of Thought
Time melts, and we are caught,
In the web of life. As our brain
Re-centers; we learn to tame

The drunken monkey called the mind,
That chases rabbits of the kind
Like specs of dust, in sunshine caught
Without a destination sought.

Follow your breath within, without
Its rise and fall, is life. No doubt.
To slow it down, exhale more
abdominally, then air will pour

Effortlessly in, to set you free
Think the words: IT BREATHS ME.

BREATHING

The only way to deal with strife
is to exhale to a count of six,
and in for 3 or 4, to fix

whatever ails, there is only air
that we need 24/7, if we care
for ourselves, it is where to begin,
for Peak Performance, you can win

the race if you prepare,
Learning to focus and care
for your reaction to distraction,
And enhance your satisfaction.

Breathing consciously with EZ-Air,
The Biofeedback Federation of Europe really care!

WILLPOWER!

Willpower implies a lack of unity,
Because DECISIONS, once made by the community
of 'Selves' - should be adhered to with ease,

Because, "Who but YOURSELF is there to please?"

THOUGHTS

After observing ones thoughts for some time
the idea of observer observed seems absurd.
And out of the chorus one voice is heard,
the sound of our thoughts, and an idea sublime,

which halts the cacophony and lets silence reign.
Like rain in the desert, or sun in a flood.
As lungs need oxygen and our hearts need blood,
The mind needs silence to remain sane.

MINDFULNESS

What can one say about Mindfulness?
When one discusses Consciousness!
It is a time to count our blessings
Like Love, Devotion, things that brings,

Out the Divine in our minds,
Beyond words, when one finds
EMOTIONS of gratitude for our being
Whole, our 'Inner Strength' seeing,

we are all connected despite illusion
of separateness, the one conclusion
Beyond Thought - to quiet our mind
And connect ourselves to the 'Divine'!

Breath out for six seconds and in for four.
Appreciate life while you explore.
Mindfulness!

CONSCIOUSNESS

Freud compartmentalized the functions of mind
into super ego, ego and id, but that kind
of model, although theoretically sound
must be view in circumstances which abound

In reality. The integrated personality reacting to stress
asserts itself for protection under duress.
man and environment must always interact
and in exceptional conditions where stimuli is lacked,

compensatory alignment is automatic
for our psyches system is never static.
Depending on perspectives a man's self-conception
can be delusional. But there is the exception.

Without trace of conceit or vanity to detect,
I'm not egotistical, I'm merely perfect.

5. REBORN AGAIN

My Rebirth-day celebratory Poem of December 10th 2020 was my First Rebirth-day, after I died twice, in 2019.

I had been in the kitchen of my office, waiting for coffee, surrounded by the Team at Thought Technology. I awoke 4 days later, and with an implanted defibrillator.

Emergency Medical Officers had saved me by defibrillating my heart twice, taking me to the Jewish General Hospital, where I was repaired.

REBIRTH-DAY CELEBRATORY POEM!

I got Defibrillated one year ago,
Twice, double lucky, as I grow
Healthy again, back in the gym
I feel like singing that old hymn

"Blessed be the Lord who reviveth the dead"
It is no longer in jest that it is said;
O.K. once was enough for Jesus the Christ;
A double blessing bestowed on me twice,

How to repay such an honour I know,
Spread Joy and Celebration as I grow
Younger each year, with gratitude on top
Of the icing on Birthday Cakes, without stop

Music and Dance, blessings galore
Makes me feel whole, to my core.

POETRY

They come out 'plop' like the egg of a bird,
or sometimes more closely related to a turd.
I don't seem to control their meter or flow,
their goal or route I vaguely know.

The first line of a couplet I might set down
and then comb the alphabet fumbling around
for a rhyme. There seems to be a predetermined order
which is useless to fight. It seems to border

Either on slovenly boredom or a gift,
'cause there's no plan and I rarely sift
my brain for a second or two at most.
Maybe I'm inhabited by a holy ghost

who makes certain my lines all rhyme.
Dammed if I know, but it happens every time.

DIVINITY POEM TO 15 YR. OLD DAUGHTER

My daughter feels that God is not,
Real, Really. But she is caught
In the existential dilemma where logic
is powerless for matters not pedagogic.

To ponder the enormity of billions of galaxies
and trillions of planets, has throughout history
Turned linear thinking into a sop.
Of mental gymnastics which cannot stop

the realization that logic and reason
are mundane tools. It is mental treason
to think that a word can encompass the whole
complexity. And that the human soul

is the end all and be all, "Oh Glorious me".
And that we are the rulers of all we can see.

MOTHER'S DAY POEM

Mothers are special - do we know why,
How about giving birth, men couldn't try,
And for feeding, they win hands down,
Men could never, so don't be a clown.

Clearly - their role is unique,
they usually teach babies to speak,
and as for affection they're number one,
Men do try, but Moms are the Sun,

That warm our lives, and make us whole,
They're what connect us to our soul,
They are our mirror, to connect us within,
They're 100% critical, unless you're a twin,

then you have to settle for fifty percent affection,
In short - they are by design, simply perfection.
Happy Mother's Day!

DON'T REVEL IN SOMEONE'S PAIN

Don't revel in someone's Pain
Even if their behavior was insane!
Manipulative, based on fomenting hate
to chase power and only to sate

appetite; trite, sexual sleaze.
Motivation only one word, greed.
Mothers' milk devoid of love
Rejecting spiritual connecting to above.

One can open ones' eyes,
To conceptually realize
Our DNA is proof that divine
plan has written this play so we define

our response to challenge and enable us to write
history; with love we can unite.

LOOK UP TO THE SKY

Look up to the Sky
Ask yourself the question: Why
are there a Billion Planets in our Galaxy
and two Trillion Galaxies - and sigh.

We are mortal, feel the call within,
Realize we need not win
Recognize our humanity
That we have divinity

Wonder what does that mean
The concept is obscene
Triumphing at life
Conquering - source of strife.

That's why when describing every single sport
Imbedded, is the word PLAY, I'm joyous to report.

WHY GO TO MARS?

Why go to Mars, what do you know,
About the environment? No Air, No
Surface Water, or WIFI, No Heat,
Life in a support tent - move your feet,

In the air, you're going nowhere with piles
Of laundry, there's Nothing for 10's of millions of miles!
Two hundred fifty thousand miles to the moon.
If you want a barren rock don't be a loon!

You're living on Mars, it's like Puerto Rico - No help
Will be coming from the US of A - you can Yelp
Like a dog, but your leash is way too long,
Your National Anthem will be your 'Swan Song',

"Oh Say can You see" - well not that 'F-ing Far'
The idiot spent 6 Billion Dollars, intelligence sub par!

ODE TO GALAXIES

100 Billion Alien Planets Fill Our Milky Way Galaxy:
The fact there's some two Trillion Galaxies,
If that's not the definition of infinite it must be close
enough for us to use it, I do suppose.

A "galactic federation" has been waiting for humans
to "reach a stage where humankind understands
what space and spaceships are" Haim Eshed,
director of space programs for Israel said.
For us to imagine; what communication we share,
What language, or vocal cord vibration do we dare,
imagine our smartphones will translate their
Beeps & Boops, to discuss their planet and keeps
them focused - sharing how to clean up Earth,
And restore Peace, for which there's a dearth.

THE DALAI LAMA POEM

The Dalai Lama for a million Smiles,
Talked about farting on a plane, Piles
Of people, thrown into Paroxysm of laughter,
Being a man of the people, he helped us infer,

His holiness, a Nobel Laureate, has gas like you or I,
In an Airplane, overcome by indigestion, he would sigh,
Driven by his urgent need to pass Wind,
He realized his humanity and that he hadn't sinned.

Most important in his eyes are one's fellow man,
Or woman, seeing the divinity within is all we can
Do to realize that creating heaven on earth,
Is within our capacity if we recognize the worth

Of young or old and realize no matter what our name,
"We are mentally, emotionally, intellectually all the same."

Laughter's the best medicine for whatever ails you, except a Hernia!

EULOGIES - LEONARD COHEN

In your Eighty-Second Year, Leonard Cohen,
Or 43rd anniversary of your 39 - wherever you roam,
A Montrealer you were, poetic and lithe,
World Class artist - you surely thrive,

In the spotlight of Art, a towering Voice,
Perhaps a bit raspy, your unique choice
Of Poetic illusions -of the human Spirit,
Uplifting - transcendent - depth and wit,

Unique is the word to capture your Song,
"Hallelujah" - rejoice - you make us belong
To our humanity, as we wander the World,
Our roots, grounded in your song. Never old.

We rejoice in the wonder you helped us discover
Accept our thanks, spiritual big brother.

EULOGIES - JEAN BÉLIVEAU

Jean Béliveau now benched for life,
A classy gentleman with no strife.
Captain of Les Canadiens,
Ten Stanley Cups, there were just eight Clubs. When

Hockey was played with Wooden Sticks,
No Helmet or Face Mask, Tricks?
Jean shot the puck into the net,
World Class balance, when he set

His shot was hot! Before Carbon Kevlar
Technology transformed newbies into a star
With grace Big Bill glided on and off the ice,
Modest, cared for his fans, just plain nice!

A legend of Hockey, Beloved by all,
We bend a Knee - you answered the call!

REST IN PEACE PRESIDENT TRUMP

Rest In Peace President Trump,
This feels like America taking a Dump,
After painful constipation of four years,
This analogy is appropriate for the tears

You've generated, for the quarter million dead,
Of your Bumbling Bull-Bleep of Covid lead.
Your Clorox suggestions, and no mask idiocy,
You're ranting to Proud Boy Nazis - we are free

Of No Global Warming, No Collusion, No Brain
Positions on digging Coal, completely insane
Cavorting with dictators, Putin & Xi,
Pretending you're leading the land of the FREE!

A tortured youth by a cold heartless Dad,
A tragic historic figure, it's really so sad.

CIVILIZATION

Civilization is hazardous to our health,
proportional usually to our wealth.
Our blood thick with chemical mystery,
Singular; the first time in our history

We are contaminated by ingenious minds
and the mass desire for all kinds
Of goodies, to produce a life of ease
And disease.

We thought we'd out psyched the system,
But our evolution links which stem
from the roots of time,
climb

To some illusory goals,
leading to the shoals
of civilization. Destiny is cosmic chaos,
for we are at a loss to pinpoint the point of it all,

Save the fall
from grace.

PLACEBO

The whole concept of Placebo is that your Mind
Is Powerful. Belief has just that kind
of ability to turn a Sugar Pill into Morphine
and eliminate Pain. Some say the concept's obscene!

It empowers belief, that transformative kind
that brings into being the concept of divine
energy within all human beings
that atheists abhor, as they like seeing

Empirical Data, like feeding a rat
the formulation and requiring that
the power be demonstrated on all levels of being
to eliminate pain. So, what you're seeing,

that curing illness can be accomplished by Psychophysiology,
Is there a contribution by placebo? So what, undoubtedly.

PHUKPHARMA

PhukPharma, you gotta know,
Your mouth is open, they're going to throw,
As many pills in as you will swallow,
Their rational is really shallow,

Return on investment, they have a stake,
In your health, for heaven's sake,
They cured Polio - and the clap,
So swallow hard, don't be a sap,

But this is where it comes off the rails,
Your good health really pales,
Compare to their need to sell some more,
So they come 'a knockin' at your door.

Direct To Consumer advertising,
DTC - it's quite surprising!

Ask Your Doctor about the Purple Pill,
Why do I need it, I'll lose my will,
To play, I was happy then I lost
the will to Pray - what's the cost.

They needed to sell healthy people a pill,
Your hair is thinning, so what if you will
Look like Yul Brenner, it could be cool,
Swallow Rogaine fill my swimming pool,

With money, cause now we have Viagra,
You'll have more sex than Lady Gaga,
Till you're eighty, ninety and some,
And here's a pill that's just for fun

'Cause reality can be a bummer,
Here's one to make winter look like summer,
Take some for ADD, so you can focus,
Anxious in crowds, don't make a fuss,

We've labeled too much reality in the DSM4,
We've got a pill for everything, except war.

Ask Your Doctor about the Purple Pill,
Why do I need it, I'll lose my will,
To play, I was happy then I lost
the will to Pray - what's the cost.

You got a TV in your hand, on an iPhone,
So no matter where you roam,
You can be in touch, there's no off switch
You're plugged in - there's just one hitch,

Sunrise, sunset, phuk that noise,
My iPods in my ears, and the joys
Of a simple life have come and gone,
It seems like I've lost my song.

Now I'm a consumer, where's my pill,
I no longer know how to just chill,
Seems like I'm wound till the breaking point,
And it's illegal to light up a joint,

So where is pharma, I'd better get a script,
From the man - till I'm in the crypt.

Ask Your Doctor about the Purple Pill,
Why do I need it, I'll lose my will,

To play, I was happy then I lost
the will to Pray - what's the cost.

Civilization 1:

Consume, Consume
'til there's no more room
to move, to breath,
we'll drill 'till we cleave
this old world in two.
Mother Nature makes a fine screw.

6. I CAN FLY

BASKETBALL POEM / SONG

Welcome to the celebration
Of Basketball, in every nation!
The Sport brings out the best in all
Individuals who answer the call

Of grounded flight, no matter how tall
All can play, it's accuracy when that ball
Makes a swoosh; and the best Team
Can fulfill everyone's dream.

For it's when the Sport becomes a dance
Down the court players prance
And pass with lightning accuracy
And we all respond with glee,

To hear our song played at the end,
And in prayer, our knees we bend!

SPORT IS FUN

"Sport is Fun" - It's repetition
Self-reinforcing, by definition
Refines, and re-establishes Balance
Body & Soul, to enhance

The tuned machine becomes aware
Of breath: to take great care
Your outbreath really does define
Your heartbeat variability, you refine,

Homeostasis by definition
Is desirable: let your condition
Be great, going with the flow of energy directed
Happiness is the objective.

Cross-fit enables you to reach the core.
And reconnect you to yourself, there is always more!

FIRST WOMAN SKIER OVER 120 MPH

Kirsten Culver, fastest woman on skis,
Two Hundred Kilometers plus, freeze
Time for an instant, thundering by,
a gorgeous gazelle, that can fly.

Behind sweet smile, nerves of steel.
Sparkling eyes gently reveal,
That fiery intensity
That makes her ski

Fast and Faster still,
How much quicker will
The snow free her to fly,
The wind allows her to slip by.

There's only one way to know,
With another run down a cliff of snow!

SKIING

Quivering Swords of Kevlar / Steel,
Flying Low and High - Repeal,
The law of Gravity - Suspend,
Time, Connect to the Joy - The End!

MIND OVER MUSCLE

Mind Over Muscle - use your mind
To enhance your experience, you know the kind
Where you're centered, confident and in the zone,
Savour your Sport, your performance you'll hone.

What word universally precedes every sport
That word, only One, I can Report
IS PLAY! Jack Donahue of Basketball fame
Coached the Canadian Olympic Team. The same

emotion: Hockey, Baseball, Football, Basketball,
we play for fun, that Joy – Recall
We were four, six, eight and ten,
In the park, field, street and when,

Our parents called, come in, dinner's on
The table. We begged for just one
More goal, hit, hike, or shot,
the game was why we played. Not

money, medal, glory or cup,
play is too much fun to interrupt.

AFTERWORD

This book has collected my dad's favourites of his so many poems. My favourites are kept in boxes and bins. A lifetime worth of memories, thoughts, and devotions that illustrate a life rich beyond measure. I hear him all the time.

- Ariella Klein

Lawrence's path to poetry began during his "meditation vacation"— a year spent in a Dutch penitentiary for marijuana possession. He described his first poems coming to him as if by divine providence — whole, complete. Poetry was his love language — how he expressed his care for his loved ones, his dismay over current events, and the small wonders and joys he found in life.

Even in his last days he continued to write poetry, having no other option, on the back of hospital menu cards.

-Talia Klein

ACKNOWLEDGEMENTS

We would like to thank publisher Howard Aster, for his commitment that created this book.

Brother Jack Klein for his introduction and energies in bringing the project to fruition.

The poetry organization and editing of daughter Talia Klein.

The graphic design and organizational skills of Tamar Peled.